The M

In Crowland

By

John Kemmery

www.fast-print.net/store.php

The Mailman in Crowland
Copyright © John Kemmery 2012

All rights reserved

No part of this book may be reproduced in any form by photocopying or any electronic or mechanical means, including information storage or retrieval systems, without permission in writing from both the copyright owner and the publisher of the book.

ISBN 978-178035-232-9

First published 2012 by
FASTPRINT PUBLISHING
Peterborough, England.

The Mailman
in Crowland

Author John Kemmery

This book was written with the permission of all the living relatives of the Middleton family and all photos and documents relating to the family were supplied by them. All other information was obtained by myself.

Contents

Introduction

Acknowledgement

Chapter 1

Mark Middleton the Mailman

Chapter 2

Lincoln Asylum

Chapter 3

Records of the Middleton Family

Chapter 4

Royal Mail in the 1800s

Chapter 5

Pictures of the Middleton Family

Introduction

This is the life story of Mark Middleton, born in Stamford, Lincolnshire in 1841, died in 1883. He was a mail cart driver for the Royal Mail. He was married to Emma Sharpe. They had nine children. Mark had an accident on Peterborough Town Bridge and after a long illness he died in Lincoln Asylum, aged 42.
This all started by reading a article in the local paper by Percy Hall which was shown to me by Mick Masters from records kept by his late wife. I contacted Mrs M. Cary. Percy Hall was her father.
She showed me all the documents that her father kept on Mark Middleton. After seeing these I suggested that it should be turned into a book.
Having been given permission in writing, and consent of the living relatives, I started to write this book. So this is the life of Mark Middleton.

Acknowledgments

Margaret Cary (née Hall), Madeline A. Brown (née Hall)
Mick Masters, Lincolnshire Archives, Peterborough Library,
Gilbert Smith.

Chapter 1
Mark Middleton the Mailman

Mark Middleton was born in 1841, in Stamford, Lincolnshire. His parents were Robert Middleton and Jane Goodwin. They were married in St Johns in Stamford, Lincolnshire in 1834. Mark was one of five children on the 1851 census, the others being Robert (16), John (13), Mary A (11) and William (3). Robert Middleton had been born in Grantham, Lincolnshire but all his children were born in Stamford; his occupation was a groom.

Mark Middleton married Emma Sharpe on 25th December, 1865 and they had ten children - Ernest Hardy (born 1869), Mark (born 1869), Ada Selina (born 1871), Robert Goodwin (born 1873), Robert Mark (born 1875), Mary (born 1877), Emily Jane (born 1879), James Herbert (born 1880), James Herbert (born 1881), Gertrude Daffarn (born 1881).

Mark Middleton worked for the Royal Mail for 16 years. He had a contract with the Royal Mail in 1876 to deliver the mail between Crowland, Thorney, Eye, Whittlesey and Peterborough by Mail Cart. He was paid £170 a year but this was later increased to £180. See Mark Middleton's contract with the Royal Mail.
His wife Emma did the day-to-day running of the Post Office in Crowland.

Mark died on 18th November 1883 in Lincoln Asylum after an accident on Peterborough Town Bridge.

His wife Emma was left to run the Post Office and mail deliveries by herself. She employed George Taylor, who had been the relief driver, to carry out the Mail Cart duties.

The house was in West Street with stables possibly at the rear of the building. I do not know if the Post Office was run from the house in West Street but this was usual practice at that time. This is all the information I could find at the time of writing this.

The Post Office was there until about 1914 when it moved to the corner of West Street and Albion Street.

In 1885 Emma married John Hall and they had two children, Dora Ethel and Sydney George.

Mary

Mark Middleton

Ernest

Emily Jane

Emma Middleton

Robert Mark

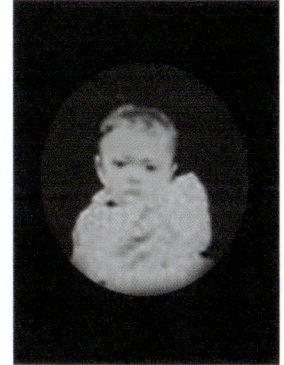
James Herbert

Ada Salina

Royal Mail driver braved danger

By PERCY HALL
Millfield Gardens,
Crowland.

TOP LEFT: The mail driver sets off from the old post office at Crowland. ABOVE: Workers pictured outside the former post office in Eye.

THESE pictures show views of Crowland and Bourne post offices, which were part of the daily route for the Bourne to Peterborough Royal Mail cart.

My grandfather Mark Middleton, who lived in West Street, Crowland was a Royal Mail contractor.

He would start work at 5pm, collecting mail from the Crowland post office before going on to Thorney and Whittlesey, eventually delivering to the general post office in Peterborough.

He also took the mail for the midnight Peterborough to London train. After a few hours sleep he would leave at 6am on the return journey, dropping the mail at Whittlesey and Thorney.

After a dull, dreary winter he always looked forward to Candlemas Day, February 2. With the days lengthening he could usually start his journey before stopping to light the candles on his cart.

The journey was made more difficult when Whittlesey Wash was flooded.

Often he travelled through the floods and when warned of danger, he replied: "I must get through with the mail."

When conditions were too bad, he made a detour via Eye-Peterborough Stanground for the Whittlesey mail.

During the day, he and the horse were on standby to pull the fire engine to any local farm stack fire.

One frosty morning, when crossing Peterborough Bridge, the horse slipped and fell, throwing Mr Middleton to the ground. He received head injuries from which he never recovered. He died on November 25, 1883, aged 42.

His widow Emma, left with a young family, employed a man called George Taylor to do the driving before marrying John Hall. The post office later closed, replaced by a new one in West Street in 1914.

Royal Mail Driver
Braved Danger

By Percy Hall
Millfield Gardens
Crowland

These pictures show Crowland and Bourne post offices, which were part of the route for the Bourne to Peterborough Royal Mail cart. My grandfather, Mark Middleton, who lived in West Street, Crowland, was a Royal Mail contractor. He would start work at 5pm, collecting mail from Crowland post office before going on to Thorney and Whittlesey, eventually delivering to the general post office in Peterborough. He also took the mail for the midnight Peterborough to London train. After a few hours sleep he would leave at 6am on the return journey, dropping the mail at Whittlesey and Thorney. After a dreary winter he always looked forward to Candlemas Day, February 2nd. With the days lengthening he could usually start his journey before stopping to light the candles on his cart. The journey was made more difficult when Whittlesey Wash was flooded. Often he travelled through the floods and when warned of danger, he replied, "I must get through with the mail." When conditions were too bad, he made a detour via Eye, Peterborough and Stanground for the Whittlesey mail. During the day the horse was on standby for the fire engine to attend any local farm stack fire.

One frosty morning when crossing Peterborough Bridge, the horse slipped and fell, throwing Mr Middleton to the ground. He received head injuries from which he never recovered. He died on 25th November, 1883, aged 42.

His widow, left with a young family, employed a man named George Taylor to do the driving. In 1885 Emma married John Hall and they had two children. The post office later closed, replaced by a new one in West Street in 1914.

Mark Middleton (Mail Man) Grandfather Born 1842 Died 1884

Mail Contractor (Crowland, Thorney, Whittlesey, Peterborough.

Tragic end to the life of a mailman

CROWLAND historian John Kemmery is looking for clues to the life of a well-regarded postal worker who met a tragic end.

MARK Middleton's life as a mailman was dangerous and ended in a desperate fashion, but his 16-year-career is now the subject of a new book. Its author John Kemmery is looking for stories and pictures from his life.

Mail cart driver Mark Middleton was born in 1841 and well-known in the Crowland area throughout his career, delivering as far as Peterborough, Eye, Thorney and Whittlesey.

But the father-of-nine suffered a serious head injury when his horses slipped on ice in an accident on Peterborough Town Bridge.

Mr Middleton was condemned to the barren surroundings of Lincoln Asylum, where he died in 1884.

Mr Kemmery is now writing a book about Mr Middleton and his wife Emma Sharpe, and hopes that "The Mailman of Crowland" will enjoy the same success as his previous book "The Jackdaws of Crowland".

That book was published last year, telling the story of the 1947 Crowland floods, and has so far raised more than £120 for the Royal British Legion Yaxley.

Appeals in the *Peterborough Evening Telegraph* and other newspapers for information, photographs and memorabilia proved successful, and Mr Kemmery is hoping for similar items for his new book.

His latest project started when he spoke to a friend called Mick Masters, who showed Mr Kemmery an article by Percy Hall – a distant relative of John Hall, the man Emma Sharpe married after Mr Middleton's death.

The article revealed some of the dangers of riding a cart by candlelight through the fens during the dark winter nights, and on at least one occasion rode through floods at Whittlesey.

Mr Kemmery said: "It seemed an interesting story and I contacted Margaret Cary, who was Percy Hall's daughter, to see if she had information.

"Inside a little tin box there were photographs of Mr Middleton and his family, and items from his life. I thought; 'there's a story here'.

"I went to the Lincolnshire Archives and they were flabbergasted that we had got the original documents, which detailed how he got £170 a year to be a mail contractor.

"His life is a story I am enthralled by."

Middleton, who was born in Stamford, delivered post for Royal Mail for 16 years, while Emma Sharpe ran the office.

One letter from 1876 shows confirmation of his acceptance to convey post between Peterborough and Crowland, in a Mail Cart which must have seats "restricted to 17 inches, to prevent the conveyance of passengers."

One particularly cold remnant is his certificate from William Sergeant of the Royal College of Physicians, certifying him as a "lunatic".

"There is incoherence with loss of memory and the reasoning faculty. He has no idea of the day or week of his birth and does not know his age.

MAILMAN OF CROWLAND: Mark Middleton with his son Robert.

"He cannot give expression to his thoughts. His gait is unsteady, he stumbles over uneven places. He has been to my house and walked through my kitchen and passages uninvited with a vacant and senseless expression."

But there are other more joyous and unusual pieces, such as the photograph of Mark's son Ernest, who had a pet fox that people could stroke if they made donations to the local football club.

Mr Middleton lived in West Street, and Mr Kemmery would particularly like a picture of the post office in that Street from the 19th century. His upcoming projects include a book on Crowland football teams from the 1930s to 1970s, an RAF plane that was shot down around the time of World War One, and a train accident at Postland Station.

For more information, or if you can help with his research, telephone 01733 700516, email john@historybuffman.co.uk, or go to www.historybuffman.co.uk.

Mark Middleton's contract

3 July 1853.

Sir,

With reference to previous correspondence, I have to inform you that your payment for the mail cart service between Peterboro' and Crowland will be raised from £170 to £180 a year on and from the 1st August next, in consideration of the new conditions imposed upon you in connexion with the introduction of the Parcel Post and on the understanding that you make such temporary alteration of your mail cart as will enable you to carry the Post office Parcels in addition to the letter mails.

You understand that the carriage of all private parcels by your cart of whatever weight, except parcels of unposted newspapers addressed to news agents, will be prohibited.

I am
Sir
Your obedient Servant

W Crowell
Surveyor, G.P.O.

Mr. Mark Middleton
Mail Contractor

Dated 3rd July 1883

Sir

With reference to previous correspondence, I have to inform you that your payment for the mail cart service between Peterborough and Crowland will be raised from £170 to £180 a year on and from the 1st August next in consideration of the new conditions imposed upon you in connexion with the introduction of the Parcel Post and on the understanding that you make such temporary alteration of your mail cart as will enable you to carry the Post Office parcels in addition to the letter mails.

You understand that the carriage of all private parcels by your cart of whatever weight, except parcels of unposted newspapers addressed to new agents, will be prohibited.

                I am
                    Sir
                    Your obedient servant

                Surveyor G P O

Mr Mark Middleton

Mail Contractor

Mark Middleton's contract

17809

11th February 1876.

Sir,

I beg to inform you that I have received the sanction of the Postmaster General to accept your Tender for the conveyance of the Mails by **Mail Cart** between **Peterborough** and **Crowland** for a payment at the rate of £170 — per annum. A Receipt for your Allowance will be sent Monthly, which can be cashed by your Banker, or by any principal Postmaster.

You will provide a Mail Cart in conformity with the Post Office Regulations as to shape, color (red), and width of the seat, which must be restricted to 17 inches, to prevent the conveyance of passengers.

You will be held strictly responsible that careful and steady Men are employed to drive the Cart, for if the Driver be reported for drunkenness, for conveying passengers, or for delaying the Mails in any way, through wilfulness or want of care, he will be prosecuted according to Law, and will incur a penalty of Twenty Pounds or Six Months' Imprisonment, for each Offence. And

17809   11th February 1876

Sir,
   I beg to inform you that I have received the sanction of the Postmaster General to accept your tender for the conveyance of the mails by mail cart between Peterborough and Crowland for a payment at the rate of £170 per annum. A receipt for your allowance will be sent monthly, which can be cashed by your banker, or by any principal postmaster.

   You will provide a mail cart in conformity with the Post Office regulations as to shape, colour (red), and width of the seat, which must be restricted to 17 inches, to prevent the conveyance of passengers.

   You will be held responsible that careful and steady men are employed to drive the cart, for if the driver be reported for drunkenness, for <u>conveying passengers,</u> or for delaying the mails in any way, through wilfulness or want of care, he will be prosecuted according to the law, and will incur a penalty of <u>twenty pounds</u> or <u>six months' imprisonment,</u> for each offence.

Mark Middleton's contract

if you knowingly employ an improper person as Driver, you expose yourself to the penalty for breach of Contract. I enclose a printed Caution on the subject.

Your Contract will commence on the 1st April next when the Cart must be ready to start from the Peterboro' Post Office at 4.0 a.m. on its route to Crowland where it must arrive by 6.30 a.m. It will be despatched from thence at 6.0 P.m. and must arrive at Peterboro' by 8.30 P.m.

These hours are liable to such alterations as the arrangements of the Department may render necessary from time to time.

Your Driver will be furnished with a Time Bill every day, and he must be strictly punctual in arriving at each Office on his route at the time stated in the Bill. He must give notice of his approach to an Office by blowing a Horn.

Mr. Mark Middleton

(Surveyors.—No. 57.)

And if you knowingly employ an improper person as driver, you expose yourself to the penalty for breach of contract. I enclose a printed caution on the subject.

Your contract will commence on the 1st April next when the cart must be ready to start from the Peterborough Post Office at 4.0 a.m. on its route to Crowland where it must arrive by 6.30 a.m. It will be despatched from thence at 6.0 p.m. And must arrive at Peterborough by 8.30 p.m.

These hours are liable to such alterations as the arrangements of the department may render necessary from time to time.

Your driver will be furnished with a Time Bill every day, and he must be strictly punctual in arriving at each office on his route at the time stated in the bill. He must give notice of his approach to an Office by blowing a horn.

Mr Mark Middleton

Mark Middleton's contract

Any further information you may require will be given to you on application at the Post Office at Peterborough

You will have the goodness to let me know, in full, your own and each of your Sureties' Names, Place of Abode, and Occupation, in order that a Contract may be prepared for the due performance of the service you have undertaken. I enclose a Form for the purpose.

I am,

Sir,

Your obedient Servant,

Charles R[...]

Surveyor to General Post Office.

Any further information you may require will be given to you on application at the Post Office at Peterborough.

You will have the goodness to let me know, in full, your own and each of your sureties' names, place of abode, and occupation, in order that a contract may be prepared for the due performance of the service you have undertaken. I enclose a form for the purpose.

        I am,
           Sir,
              Your obedient servant,

Surveyor to General Post Office

Death of the old Mailman

About a year ago Mark Middleton, the driver of the Mail Cart from Croyland through Thorney and Whittlesey to Peterborough was thrown out of his trap and his skull fractured. At first he appeared to be recovering, but he gradually lost power of both body and mind and about six weeks since he was removed from Croyland to Lincoln Asylum. He gradually got worse and died last week. His remains were brought home, and on the 29th were interred in the graveyard of the Abbey, by the Revd. T. H. Le Bauf. Deceased had been Mail Contractor and Driver 16 years, and was greatly respected for the efficient way in which he filled his important public office. Officials from the post-Office at Peterbrough attended the funeral

Death of the old Mailman

About a year ago Mark Middleton, the driver of the mail cart from Croyland through Thorney and Whittlesey to Peterborough was thrown out of his trap and his skull fractured. At first he appeared to be recovering, but he gradually lost power of both body and mind and about six weeks since he was removed from Croyland to Lincoln Asylum. He gradually got worse and died last week. His remains were brought home, and on the 29th were interred in the graveyard of the Abbey, by the Rev T H Le Boeuf. Deceased had been Mail Contractor and Driver 16 years, and greatly respected for the efficient way in which he filled his important public office. Officials from the Post Office of Peterborough attended the funeral as did also many of his townsmen, and the greatest sympathy is felt for his wife and numerous children.

Crowland Post Office 1861
Extract from the Stamford Mercury
20th December, 1861

CROWLAND.—Two sermons in aid of the Peterboro' Dispensary were preached in the Abbey church on Sunday last, by the Rev. W. Campe, M.A., Canon of Peterboro', when 5l. 16s. 1½d. was collected.

Post-office Savings Bank.—One of these useful institutions was opened at Crowland on the 9th inst. Several depositors have availed themselves of the benefits offered, and doubtless many more will as the advantages become more generally known.

The Abbey.—Workmen have been engaged in erecting scaffolding to the tower of the Abbey, for the purpose of re-fixing the weather vane, blown down by the gale a few weeks ago. The old vane has been up nearly 80 years.

J. Freeman (my wife's granddad) pictured in Eye
Mail Contractor, 1910, Eye, Newborough, Peakirk, Peterborough

Freeman family (four generations) in West Street, Eye

4632

Name Mark Middleton

Date of Admission 17th Oct 1883

Chargeable to Peterborough

ORDER FOR THE RECEPTION OF A PAUPER PATIENT.—Sched. (F.) No. 1.

(a) I Thomas James Walker the undersigned, having called to my assistance a (b) Surgeon and having personally examined Mark Middleton a Pauper, and being satisfied that the said Mark Middleton is a (c) lunatic (d) _____ and a proper person to be taken charge of and detained under Care and Treatment, hereby direct you to receive the said Mark Middleton as a Patient in your Asylum

Subjoined is a statement respecting the said Mark Middleton

Signed, Name, (e) Thomas James Walker
Justice of the Peace for the Borough of Peterborough
Name, (f) Samuel Dodson
Relieving Officer

Dated the Seventeenth Day of October One Thousand Eight Hundred and eighty-three.

To Dr. Palmer,
Resident Physician and Superintendent of the Asylum
for the County of Lincoln.

STATEMENT.

[If any Particulars in this Statement be not known, the Fact to be so stated.]

Name of Patient, with Christian Name at Length	Mark Middleton
Sex and age	Male 42
Married, Single, or Widowed	Married
Condition of Life, and previous Occupation (if any)	Mail Driver & Contractor
The Religious Persuasion, as far as known	Church of England
Previous Place of Abode	Crowland
Whether first Attack	Yes
Age (if known) on First Attack	42
When and where previously under Care and Treatment	Not anywhere
Duration of Existing Attack	Some months
Supposed Cause	Accident — fall from trap
Whether subject to Epilepsy	No
Whether Suicidal	No
Whether Dangerous to others	Yes at times
Parish or Union to which the Lunatic is chargeable	Common Fund Peterboro' Union
Name and Christian Name, and Place of Abode of nearest known Relative of the Patient, and Degree of Relationship, if known	Emma Middleton (Wife) West St Crowland

I certify that, to the best of my knowledge, the above Particulars are correctly stated.

Signed, Name, (g) Samuel Dodson R.O. of Peterborough Union. Eye. Peterborough

N.B.—To render these documents valid it is necessary that all the requirements stated in the foot-notes should be strictly complied with.

(a) I, C. D., in the case of a single Justice of the Peace; or, in the case of two Justices, or of a Clergyman and Relieving Officer or Overseer, We, C.D. and E. F.
(b) Physician, surgeon, or apothecary, as the case may be.
(c) Lunatic, an idiot, or a person of unsound mind.
(d) Add where the lunatic is sent as being wandering at large, the words "wandering at large:" and in the case of a lunatic sent by virtue of the authority given to two Justices, add, "not under proper care and control," or "and is cruelly treated [or neglected] by the person having the care or charge of him," as may appear to the Justices to be the case.
(e) Justice of the peace for the city or borough of———; or an or the officiating clergyman of the parish of———. To be signed by two Justices where required by the foregoing Act.
(f) The relieving officer of the union or parish of——— or an overseer of the parish of———.
(g) Relieving officer or overseer of the union or parish of———.

Order for the reception of a pauper patient

(a) Thomas James Walker
The undersigned having called to my assistance a (b) surgeon and having personally examined Mark Middleton is a (c) lunatic (d) and a proper person to be taken charge of and detained under care and treatment, hereby direct you to receive the said Mark Middleton as a patient in your asylum on the 17th October, 1883.
To Dr Palmer
Resident Physician and Superintendent of the Asylum for the county of Lincoln.

MEDICAL CERTIFICATE.—Sched. (F.) No. 3.

I, the undersigned, William Robert Sergeant being a (a) Licentiate of the Royal College of Physicians & Surgeons, Edin and being in actual practice as a (b) Surgeon hereby certify, that I, on the fourteenth day of October 1883, at (c) West Street Crowland in the County of Lincoln,

(d) personally examined Mark Middleton of (e) West Street, Crowland, Mail contractor and that the said Mark Middleton is a (f) Lunatic and a proper Person to be taken Charge of and detained under Care and Treatment; and that I have formed this opinion upon the following grounds, viz.:—

1. Facts indicating Insanity observed by myself (g) There is incoherence with loss of memory & the reasoning faculty — He has no idea of the day of the week or month, & does not know his age — He cannot give expression to his thoughts. His gait is unsteady, he stumbles over uneven places. He will not sit or lie long. I have seen him go to bed & get up again in five minutes & come into the kitchen of his house in his shirt. He has been to my house & walked through my kitchen & passages uninvited with a vacant & senseless expression.

2. Other facts (if any) indicating Insanity communicated to me by others (h) Emma Middleton (his wife) & Mary Parkinson (nurse) state that his actions & general behaviour are senseless. During the night he will not lie long in bed, but is frequently getting up & wandering about the house, will go into the kitchen & stand there for fifteen or twenty minutes, & into the nurse's or children's bedroom. His neighbours have seen him in the yard in his shirt. His wife has to feed him as he will not put the food to his mouth himself.

Signed, Name, Wm R Sergeant.
Place of Abode, Crowland.
Dated this fourteenth Day of October One Thousand Eight Hundred and eighty-three.

(a) Here set forth the qualification in full entitling the person certifying to practise as a physician, surgeon, or apothecary, ex. gr.:— Fellow of the Royal College of Physicians in London.
(b) Physician, surgeon, or apothecary, as the case may be.
(c) Here insert the street and number of the house (if any) or other like particulars, of the place where the examination was made. If a Pauper Lunatic be examined at a Workhouse, of which he is a Regular Inmate, the fact of his being so resident should be stated, and not merely that he was examined at the Workhouse. If he be only a Casual Inmate, his previous, or ordinary place of abode should be inserted.
(d) In any case where more than one medical certificate is required by this Act, here insert, separately from any other practitioner.
(e) Here insert residence and profession or occupation (if any).
(f) Lunatic, or an idiot, or a person of unsound mind.
(g) Here state the facts.
(h) Here state the information and from whom.

N.B.—To render this document valid it is necessary that all the requirements stated in the foot-notes should be strictly complied with.

MEDICAL CERTIFICATE

I, the undersigned, William Robert Sergeant, being a Licentiate of the Royal College of Physicians and Surgeons Edinburgh and been in actual practice as surgeon hereby certify that I on the fourteenth day of October 1883 at West Street, Crowland in the County of Lincoln personally examined Mark Middleton of West Street, Crowland, mail contractor and that the said Mark Middleton is a lunatic and a proper person to be taken charge of and detained under care and treatment and that I have formed this opinion upon the following grounds.

1. Facts indicating insanity observed by myself (g). There is incoherence with loss of memory and the reasoning faculty. He has no idea of the day of the week or his birth and does not know his age. He cannot give expression to his thoughts. His gait is unsteady, he stumbles over uneven places. He will not sit long, I have seen him go to bed and get up again in five minutes and come into the kitchen of his house in his shirt. He has been to my house & walked through my kitchen & passages uninvited with a vacant and senseless expression.
2. Other facts (if any) indicating insanity communicated to me by others (h) Emma Middleton (his wife) and Mary Parkinson (nurse) state that his actions and

MEDICAL CERTIFICATE

general behaviour are senseless. During the night, he will not lie long in bed, but is frequently getting up and wandering about the house, will go into the kitchen and stand there for fifteen or twenty minutes, and into the nurse's or children's bedroom. His neighbours have seen him in the yard in his shirt. His wife has to feed him as he will not put the food to his mouth himself.

Signed
Name W. R. Sergeant
Place Crowland dated this fourteenth day of October one thousand eight hundred and eighty three.

| Form and Character of Mental Disorder, and accompanying Bodily Disease, if any, on Admission; and Records of Medical and Moral Treatment, and progress of the Patient after Admission. | There is no history of insanity or intemperance in the family. Had a heavy fall on the head about 18 months ago since which time he has been incapacitated from following his occupation. Has a large scar on the right side of the head — Dementia with Genl. Paralysis A. Ward & Surgl. Bone |

He is low nourished, but superseded by general paralysis. Black hair, very dark hazel eyes. Left pupil larger than its fellow and fixed — Tongue dirtily, clean and tremulous — Pulse thready & habitually. He is dull and confused and has no idea where he is or how long he has been here — His habits are wet and dirty. He is usually restless at night and often unable to answer any query. He can just manage to walk a bit shortly but with an uncertain step — facial muscles are very tremulous and his deglutition is very weak — has to be fed by the spoon with sloppy diet.

November 17th. About a fortnight since he became very helpless and could not stand. He was also vacant &

There is no history of insanity or malingering in the family. Had a heavy fall on the head about 18 months ago since which time he has been incapacitated from following his occupation.

Has a large scar on the right side of the head. Dementia with good parole a ward plus single room. He is also excitable but enfeebled by general paralysis, black hair very dark, hazel eyes left pupil larger than its fellow and ….clear and mentally he … and confused and has no idea where he is or how long he has been here. His habits are … wet and dirty, he is usually restless at night and often unable to answer any queries he can just manage to walk a little … but with an uncertain steps facial muscles on .. Are very senseless and his … is very weak. Has to be fed by the spoon with a slop diet. November 11th about a fortnight since he became very helpless and could not stand; he was vacant…

1883

confused and unable to trouble any answer to inquiries. He also took very little food and with the greatest difficulty and the saliva was threaded. He was kept in bed for several days and as the bowels were constipated he was given castor oil which had to be followed up by an enema. After the bowels had been freely relieved he generally became a little clearer mentally and he would answer to simple queries and pass off daily. He cannot stand on his legs at all or in any way help himself. He extends his arms freely & this act is performed better than any other muscular movement. Has no push in the head. — Habits wet and dirty —

November 24th. Early yesterday morning he was seized with epileptiform convulsions affecting the right side of the face and body and he was quite unconscious, and during the whole day he could not swallow. The twitching continues to day but in slight in degree, and though he does not speak he looks about him and appears to be conscious. Has taken only half an ounce of liquid to day — has been very wet and dirty.

November 25th. He became suddenly much worse this morning and continued unconscious all the forenoon till he died at 2.25 p.m.

Died November 25th 1883
"Of General Paralysis of an
"grave duration."

Post mortem
examination
refused by the
relations

J.W. Ward

Confused and unable to make any answer to enquiries, he also took very little food and with the greatest difficulty and pulse was thread. He was kept in bed for several days as the bowels were constipated; he was given castor oil which had to be followed up by an enema. After the bowels had been freely relieved he gradually became a little clearer mentally and he now answers simple queries and gets up daily. He cannot stand on his legs at all or in any way help himself, he extends his arms finely & in this act performed better than any other muscular movement.
Has no pain in the head – habits wet and dirty.

November 24th early yesterday morning seized with ? affecting the right side of his face and he was quite unconscious, and during the whole day he could not swallow. The twitching continues today but is slight in degree, and although he does not speak he looks about him and appears to be conscious. Has taken only half an ounce of liquid today – he has been very wet and dirty.

November 25th - He became suddenly much worse this morning and continued unconscious all the forenoon till he died at 2.25 pm.

Died November 25th 1883
Of general paralysis of one year's duration.

Post Morton examination referred by the relations.

DROVE HORSE DRAWN MAIL CART

Mr. Herbert Middleton, of Holbeach, a native of Crowland, and a member of a well-known family, has died aged 79 years.

Older residents of Crowland and Holbeach will remember him driving the horse-drawn mail cart.

Mr. Middleton served in the 1914-1918 war with the Royal Artillery in Africa. For many years he was a member of the Holbeach Town Band.

More recently he had become a bowls player. Always a keen cyclist, he visited his home town regularly on his bicycle.

HIS FAMILY RAN ROYAL MAIL CART

THE funeral took place at Crowland Abbey of Mr. Robert Mark Middleton, aged 82, who died at his home in Lincoln.

A native of Crowland, Bob Middleton as he was affectionately known, was a member of the Middleton family who were associated with the running of the "Royal Mail Cart" between Thorney, Crowland, Whittlesey and Peterborough in the earlier days.

The possessor of a keen sence of humour, he was well known for the stories he could tell of journeys over flooded Whittlesey Wash when on the mail run. He had a keen interest in sport and was a familiar figure at most sporting events, right up to leaving Crowland.

The service was conducted by the Rector (the Rev. C. I. Lee) and the mourners were, Mrs. E. Butler, Mr. H. Middleton, Mrs. A. Locke, Mrs. E. Jennings, Mr. S. Hall (brothers and sisters); Mr. and Mrs. Len Hall, Mr. and Mrs. P. Hall, Mrs. F. Jelly, Mr. and Mrs. A. Shepherd, Mrs. B. Browning, Mr. and Mrs. E. Day, Mr. and Mrs. F. Body, Mr. and Mrs. Leslie Hall, Mrs. S. Mountney (nephews and nieces); Miss D. Scorah, Mrs. F. Herrick, Mrs. A. Adams Lincoln, Miss Margaret Hall, Miss Madelene Hall, Mr. and Mrs. W. Taylor, Mrs. A. Smith, Mr. and Mrs. H. King, Mr. F. Avery, Miss E. Freeman, Mr. R. Strickland, Mr. M. Strickland, Mrs. Coles.

Mr. G. Baldock, Lincoln, was unable to attend.

Laid to rest. — The funeral took place at the Abbey on Saturday of Mr. Robert Mark Middleton, a native of Crowland who died at his home in Lincoln at the age of 82. 'Bob' Middleton, as he was affectionately known, was a member of the family associated with the running of the Royal Mail Cart between Thorney, Crowland, Whittlesey and Peterborough. He had a keen sense of humour and was well known for the stories he could tell of journeys over flooded Whittlesey Wash when on the 'Mail Run.' He was a familiar figure at most sporting events, until leaving Crowland. The funeral service was conducted by the Rector (the Rev. C. I. Lee) and mourners were Mrs. E. Butler, Mr. H. Middleton, Mrs. A. Locke, Mrs. E. Jennings and Mr. S. Hall (brothers and sisters), Mr. and Mrs. Len Hall, Mr. and Mrs. P. Hall, Mrs. F. Jelley, Mr. and Mrs. A. Shepherd, Mrs. B. Browning, Mr. and Mrs. E. Day, Mr. and Mrs. F. Body, Mr. and Mrs. Leslie Hall and Mrs. S. Mountney (nephews and nieces), Miss D. Scorah, Mrs. F. Herrick, Mrs. A. Adams, Lincoln, Miss Margaret Hall, Miss Madeline Hall, Mr. and Mrs. W. Taylor, Mrs. A. Smith, Mr. and Mrs. H. King, Mr. F. Avery, Miss E. Freeman, Mr. R. Strickland, Mr. M. Strickland and Mrs. Coles.

THE Funeral took place on Tuesday afternoon, at the Abbey of Mr. John Hall, a native of Crowland, who died at Peterborough, on Friday, at the age of 74 years. For several years deceased was a member of the Abbey Choir and also did duty as a mail-man. He left Crowland about six years ago. The Rector, Rev. G. D. K. Clowes, officiated in the presence of the bereaved family and, amongst those present, were: Mr. Sydney Hall, Peterborough, Mrs. W. Jennings, March (son and daughter), Master Leslie Hall, Peterborough (grandson), Mr. Samuel Hall and Mrs. E. Jeffrey, London (brother and sister), Mr. T. Hall, London (brother), Miss E. Hall, Peterborough (granddaughter), Mr. Joshua Hall (brother), Miss Sylvia Hall, Peterborough (granddaughter), Mr. R. Middleton, Lincoln, Mrs. E. Butler, Peterborough, Mr. H. Middleton, Holbeach, Mrs. G. Lock, Peterborough, Mr. E. Butler, Mrs. E. Hall, Farcet, Miss M. Butler and Miss E. Butler, Peterborough, Mr. and Mrs. L. Hall, Mr. Percy Hall, Miss F. Lock, Peterborough, Mr. J. Sharpe, Miss M. Bottomley, Eye, Mr. M. Strickland, Mr. F. Maddison, Mr. J. H. Beeken, Mr. R. Strickland and Mr. G. P. Strickland. Owing to illness Mrs. S. Hall, Peterborough, and Mrs. J. Hall were unable to attend the last sad rites. The floral tributes were from: Syd, Annie and Family (Peterborough); Ethel, Will and Family (March); Brother Tom and Sister Emily (London); Brother Sam and Family; Brother Josh, Ada, Herbert, Percy and May; Bob and Nell (Lincoln); Ern' and Emily; Clara; Gertie, Alf and Family; Madge and Elsie; Laura, Harry and Family; Cecil and Elsie; Laurie; Len, Ivy and Little Ernest; Will and Gwen Robinson; Harold and Ivy; Mr. and Mrs. Emery.

EMMA (NÉE) SHARPE — MIDDLETON — HALL.

MARRIED MARK MIDDLETON.

CHILDREN:

	MARRIED		GRANDCHILDREN
ERNEST HARDY	CLARA		LAUREL
ADA SELINA	JOSHUA HALL of CROWLAND		REGINALD — CECIL, LEONARD, PERCY. DIED 1918 AGED 18. — DIED 26/6/1957 AS ON GRAVESTONE IN ABBEY CHURCHYARD
ROBERT MARK	NELL of LINCOLN		NO CHILDREN.
EMILY JANE	ERNEST BUTLER of PETERBOROUGH		MARJORIE, ELSIE. (MADGE)
HERBERT	ELIZABETH of SPALDING		ERNEST, LAUREL.
GERTRUDE	ALF LOCKE of PETERBOROUGH		LEN, GERTIE, CLARA, EVA, FLORRIE, ROLAND.
MARY	FRANK WILLIAMS of GOREFIELD		FRANK, FRED, BESSIE.

MARK MIDDLETON — DIED 25/11/1883 AS ON GRAVESTONE IN ABBEY CHURCHYARD.

EMMA MARRIED JOHN HALL — HER SON-IN-LAW JOSHUA'S BROTHER.

CHILDREN:

	MARRIED		GRANDCHILDREN.
ETHEL	WILLIAM JENNINGS of MARCH		SYDNEY, FREDA.
SYDNEY	ANNIE of LONDON		ETHEL, SYLVIA, LESLIE.

EMMA DIED 1922.

41

Emma Sharpe
Emma married Mark Middleton
25th Dec 1865

Children
Ernest Hardy married Clara Richards

Children
Laura Bessie.
Ada Selina married Joshua Hall.

Children
Reginald, Cecil, Leonard, Percy.
Reginald died 1918 aged 18.
Robert Mark married Nell (no children).
Robert died in 1957 buried in Crowland Abbey, Lincolnshire.
Emily Jane married Ernest Butler

Children
Marjorie (Madge), Elise.
Herbert married Elizabeth More

Children
Ernest, Laurel.
Gertrude married Alf Locke

Children
Len, Gertie, Clara, Eva, Florrie, Roland.
Mary married Frank Williams

Children
Frank, Fred, Bessie.

Mark Middleton died in 1883 and is buried in Crowland Abbey, Lincolnshire.

Emma Sharpe
Emma married John Hall
in 1885

Emma married John Hall (after Mark Middleton's death in 1883).

Children,
Ethel, married William Jennings

Children
Sydney, Freda.
Sydney married Annie

Children
Ethel, Sylvia, Leslie.

Emma died in 1922

Chapter 2
Lincoln Asylum

Robert Gardiner Hill (1811–1878)
House surgeon (resident medical officer) Lincoln Asylum, 1835–40; joint owner of Eastgate House Asylum Lincoln, 1840–63, and from 1863 Earls Court House Asylum, Old Brompton, London, Wyke House and Inverness Lodge, Brentford, Middlesex. Originator of the non-restraint system in lunacy.

Dr Samuel Tuke

Dr Tuke spoke of the "renaissance of humane treatment", referring to the work of Dr R. Gardiner Hill and his experiments in removing instruments of restraint at Lincoln Asylum.

St John's Asylum was built in 1852 in Bracebridge Parish on the road to Sleaford.
It was built to house 250 inmates then it was enlarged in 1859,1866,1881 and 1902. The asylum covered 120 acres.
The asylum was designed by John. R. Hamilton of Gloucester and assisted by Thomas Percy who was the surveyor to the County of Kesteven.

The grounds of the Asylum were cultivated by the inmates to provide vegetables for meals for the inmates and staff.
All the sewage from the asylum was disposed of by irrigation over ten acres of land about half a mile away from the asylum. Also the asylum had a cemetery and mortuary chapel; it covered one and a half acres of land. The inmates of Lincoln Asylum referred to it as the "Visitors".

The pictures show the mortuary chapel (below) and the church before it was demolished (above). Records do not say whether they were left and protected as listed buildings.

This chapter is about St John's Lunatic Asylum in Bracebridge Heath in Lincolnshire, where Mark Middleton spent the last months of his life.

He was sent to St John's in about 1881/2. This picture shows where Mark Middleton lived and spent his last days before his death in 1883.

This picture shows the conditions inside the asylum and what it would be like to have been a inmate.

The asylum was closed in 1990 and it was sold to a property developer which constructed nearly a thousand new homes on the site. The original hospital buildings themselves are classified as Grade III listed buildings and are protected from demolition.

During the redevelopment of the hospital site a number of these protected buildings were refurbished and converted into flats and offices.

Pictures of Lincoln Asylum St John's
Bracebridge Heath
in the 1800s before it was demolished.

Records of St. John's Hospital Bracebridge, formerly the Lincolnshire County Lunatic Asylum. It was built in 1852 and enlarged on several subsequent occasions. It was originally established jointly by Lindsey, Kesteven, Holland, Lincoln, Grimsby, and Stamford and managed by a Board of Visitors appointed by the contributing authorities. Kesteven and Grantham withdrew from the arrangement when the contract of Union expired in 1893 (eventually establishing the Kesteven County Asylum at South Rauceby,1897).

The hospital was set in grounds of 120 acres which included gardens, farmland and a burial ground. In 1940 female patients were transferred to other hospitals, mainly Stores Hall near Huddersfield, to make space for an Emergency Hospital, and many did not return until well after the end of the War. Administration of the hospital passed to the National Health Service in 1948. By the early 1960s it was known by its final name St John's Hospital. Patients were admitted from Harmston Hall Hospital when that hospital closed. St. John's Hospital itself was closed in December 1989 with the remaining patients transferred to other establishments. The site was sold for housing and most of the buildings, apart from the central block, were demolished.

The following names, among others, were used for the Institution, sometimes interchangeably:

1852-1893 Lincolnshire County Lunatic Asylum or Lincolnshire County Pauper Lunatic Asylum.
1894-1915 Lincolnshire Lunatic Asylum.
1897-1898 Lindsey, Holland, Lincoln and Grimsby District Pauper Lunatic Asylum.
1903-1920 Lincolnshire Asylum.
1898-1902 Bracebridge Pauper Lunatic Asylum.
1902-1919 Bracebridge District Lunatic Asylum.
1919-1948 Bracebridge Mental Hospital.
1930-1938 Lincolnshire Mental Hospital.
1939-1960 Bracebridge Heath Hospital.
1961-1989 St. John's Hospital, Bracebridge Heath.

The hospital was also used as an Emergency Wartime Hospital in the period 1940-1943 and a few records of this function survive with the asylum records.

Pictures of Lincoln Asylum St John's
Bracebridge Heath
in the 1800s before it was demolished

Pictures of Lincoln Asylum St John's
Bracebridge Heath
in the 1800s before it was demolished

Pictures of Lincoln Asylum St John's
Bracebridge Heath
in the 1800s before it was demolished

Pictures of Lincoln Asylum St John's
Bracebridge Heath
in the 1800s before it was demolished

Chapter 3
Records of the Middleton Family
CENSUS RECORDS OF MARK MIDDLETON

Mark Middleton and Emma Sharpe Family

Record Type	Baptism Date	Surname	Forename	County	Place
Baptisms	22 Aug 1869	MIDDLETON	Ernest Hardy	Lincolnshire	Crowland
Baptisms	22 Aug 1869	MIDDLETON	Mark	Lincolnshire	Crowland
Baptisms	23 Apr 1871	MIDDLETON	Ada Selina	Lincolnshire	Crowland
Baptisms	14 May 1873	MIDDLETON	Robert Goodwin	Lincolnshire	Crowland
Baptisms	27 Jun 1875	MIDDLETON	Robert Mark	Lincolnshire	Crowland
Baptisms	15 Sep 1877	MIDDLETON	Mary	Lincolnshire	Crowland
Baptisms	27 Apr 1879	MIDDLETON	Emily Jane	Lincolnshire	Crowland
Baptisms	04 Oct 1880	MIDDLETON	James Herbert	Lincolnshire	Crowland
Baptisms	27 Mar 1881	MIDDLETON	James Herbert	Lincolnshire	Crowland
Baptisms	25 Dec 1881	MIDDLETON	Gertrude Daffarn	Lincolnshire	Crowland

Ernest Hardy Middleton
Married Dec 1891 to Clara Richards died 1942
Children Laura Middleton

County	Lincolnshire
Place	Crowland
Church	Sts Mary Bartholomew and Guthlac
RegisterNumber	2450
DateOfBirth	
BaptismDate	22 Aug 1869
Forename	Ernest Hardy
Sex	M
FatherForename	Mark
MotherForename	Emma
FatherSurname	MIDDLETON
MotherSurname	
Abode	Croyland
FatherOccupation	mail driver
Notes	ceremony performed by W H Jackson
FileNumber	13829

Mark Middleton Died 1870 8mths old

County	Lincolnshire
Place	Crowland
Church	Sts Mary Bartholomew and Guthlac
RegisterNumber	2451
DateOfBirth	
BaptismDate	22 Aug 1869
Forename	Mark
Sex	M
FatherForename	Mark
MotherForename	Emma
FatherSurname	MIDDLETON
MotherSurname	
Abode	Croyland
FatherOccupation	mail driver
Notes	ceremony performed by W H Jackson
FileNumber	13829

Ada Selina Middleton Married Joshua Hall 1900
Children Ernest Reginald

County	Lincolnshire
Place	Crowland
Church	Sts Mary Bartholomew and Guthlac
RegisterNumber	2549
DateOfBirth	
BaptismDate	23 Apr 1871
Forename	Ada Selina
Sex	F
FatherForename	Mark
MotherForename	Emma
FatherSurname	MIDDLETON
MotherSurname	
Abode	Croyland
FatherOccupation	mail driver
Notes	ceremony performed by G K Perry
FileNumber	13829

Robert Goodwin Middleton Died 1873 4mths old

County	Lincolnshire
Place	Crowland
Church	Sts Mary Bartholomew and Guthlac
RegisterNumber	2640
DateOfBirth	
BaptismDate	14 May 1873
Forename	Robert Goodwin
Sex	M
FatherForename	Mark
MotherForename	Emma
FatherSurname	MIDDLETON
MotherSurname	
Abode	Chapel St Croyland
FatherOccupation	mail clerk driver
Notes	ceremony performed by C B Hulbert
FileNumber	13829

County	Lincolnshire
Place	Crowland
Church	Sts Mary Bartholomew and Guthlac
RegisterNumber	2751
DateOfBirth	
BaptismDate	27 Jun 1875
Forename	Robert Mark
Sex	M
FatherForename	Mark
MotherForename	Emma
FatherSurname	MIDDLETON
MotherSurname	
Abode	Croyland
FatherOccupation	poultry dealer
Notes	ceremony performed by J Curry
FileNumber	13829

County	Lincolnshire
Place	Crowland
Church	Sts Mary Bartholomew and Guthlac
RegisterNumber	2866
DateOfBirth	
BaptismDate	15 Sep 1877
Forename	Mary
Sex	F
FatherForename	Mark
MotherForename	Emma
FatherSurname	MIDDLETON
MotherSurname	
Abode	Croyland
FatherOccupation	mail contracter
Notes	ceremony performed by J Curry
FileNumber	13829

Emily Jane Middleton Married Ernest Butler 1904

County	Lincolnshire
Place	Crowland
Church	Sts Mary Bartholomew and Guthlac
RegisterNumber	2939
DateOfBirth	
BaptismDate	27 Apr 1879
Forename	Emily Jane
Sex	F
FatherForename	Mark
MotherForename	Emma
FatherSurname	MIDDLETON
MotherSurname	
Abode	Croyland
FatherOccupation	mail cart driver
Notes	ceremony performed by Francis A Godfrey
FileNumber	13829

County	Lincolnshire
Place	Crowland
Church	Sts Mary Bartholomew and Guthlac
RegisterNumber	3007
DateOfBirth	15 Sep 1880
BaptismDate	27 Mar 1881
Forename	James Herbert
Sex	M
FatherForename	Mark
MotherForename	Emma
FatherSurname	MIDDLETON
MotherSurname	
Abode	New Road
FatherOccupation	mail cart driver
Notes	ceremony performed by T H Le Boeuf publicly received this day see No 2983
FileNumber	13829

County	Lincolnshire
Place	Crowland
Church	Sts Mary Bartholomew and Guthlac
RegisterNumber	2983
DateOfBirth	15 Sep 1880
BaptismDate	04 Oct 1880
Forename	James Herbert
Sex	M
FatherForename	Mark
MotherForename	Emma
FatherSurname	MIDDLETON
MotherSurname	
Abode	New Road
FatherOccupation	mail cart driver
Notes	ceremony performed by Thomas Henry Le Boeuf
FileNumber	13829

Gertrude Daffarn Middleton Married Alfred Lock 1906

County	Lincolnshire
Place	Crowland
Church	Sts Mary Bartholomew and Guthlac
RegisterNumber	3029
DateOfBirth	08 Nov 1881
BaptismDate	25 Dec 1881
Forename	Gertrude Daffarn
Sex	F
FatherForename	Mark
MotherForename	Emma
FatherSurname	MIDDLETON
MotherSurname	
Abode	West St Croyland
FatherOccupation	mail cart driver
Notes	ceremony performed by Thomas Henry Le Boeuf
FileNumber	13829

Dora Ethel Hall children of Emma Hall and John Hall Emma (Second Marriage)

County	Lincolnshire
Place	Crowland
Church	Sts Mary Bartholomew and Guthlac
RegisterNumber	3154
DateOfBirth	24 May 1885
BaptismDate	29 Nov 1885
Forename	Dora Ethel
Sex	F
FatherForename	John
MotherForename	Emma
FatherSurname	HALL
MotherSurname	
Abode	Croyland
FatherOccupation	mail cart driver
Notes	ceremony performed by T H Le Boeuf
FileNumber	13996

Sydney George children of Emma Hall and John Hall Emma (Second Marriage)

County	Lincolnshire
Place	Crowland
Church	Sts Mary Bartholomew and Guthlac
RegisterNumber	3200
DateOfBirth	10 Apr 1887
BaptismDate	28 Aug 1887
Forename	Sydney George
Sex	M
FatherForename	John
MotherForename	Emma
FatherSurname	HALL
MotherSurname	
Abode	Crowland
FatherOccupation	mail cart driver
Notes	ceremony performed by T H Le Boeuf
FileNumber	13996

CERTIFIED COPY OF AN ENTRY OF BIRTH

GIVEN AT THE GENERAL REGISTER OFFICE,
SOMERSET HOUSE, LONDON

Application Number PK 8279/68

BIRTH in the Sub-district of Stamford in the Counties of Lincoln etc.

1910

No.	When and where born	Name, if any	Sex	Name, and surname of father	Name, surname, and maiden surname of mother	Occupation of father	Signature, description, and residence of informant	When registered	Signature of registrar	Name entered after registration
	Thirtieth March 1910 44 Priesty's Buildings Scotgate Stamford U.D.	Ernest Prince MacDonald	Boy	Herbert James Middleton	Isabel Jane Middleton formerly Jackson	Groom (domestic)	I.J. Middleton mother 6 Priesty's Buildings Scotgate Stamford	Fourth May 1910	R.J. Chicess Registrar	

CERTIFIED to be a true copy of an entry in the certified copy of a Register of Births in the District above mentioned.
Given at the GENERAL REGISTER OFFICE, SOMERSET HOUSE, LONDON, under the Seal of the said Office, the 17th day of July, 1968.

BX 524171

*See note overleaf

R.B.D.

CERTIFIED COPY OF AN ENTRY
Pursuant to the Births and Deaths Registration Act 1953

DEATH

Entry Number 189

Registration District **Peterborough**
Sub-district **Peterborough**

Administrative area County of **Cambridgeshire**

1. Date and place of death
Twenty-sixth August 1993
Found dead on arrival at District Hospital, Peterborough

2. Name and surname
Ernest Mark McDonald MIDDLETON

3. Sex Male

4. Maiden surname of woman who has married

5. Date and place of birth
30th March 1910 Stamford Lincolnshire

6. Occupation and usual address
Lorry Driver (retired)
35 Wootton Avenue Old Fletton Peterborough Cambs.

7. (a) Name and surname of informant
Tony McDonald MIDDLETON

(b) Qualification
Son
In attendance

(c) Usual address
92 Lawson Avenue Stanground Peterborough Cambs.

8. Cause of death
1a. Ruptured Atherosclerotic Abdominal Aortic Aneurysm

Certified by G.S.Ryall Coroner for Peterborough after post mortem without inquest

9. I certify that the particulars given by me above are true to the best of my knowledge and belief.
T.M.Middleton

Signature of informant

10. Date of registration
Thirty-first August 1993

11. Signature of registrar
Mary Helsby Registrar

Certified to be a true copy of an entry in a register in my custody.
Mary Helsby .... Registrar 31.8.1993 . Date

IAG 012428

Reminiscences by Irene Challenger

Granddaughter of Ernest Middleton
I picked out a few pieces from her reminiscences of Ernest Middleton's life.

Ernest joined the postal service in London as a telegram delivery boy aged about 14years old and later became a postman (mailman). He worked for the Royal Mail until he was sixty years old.

Ernest had lots of hobbies, one being an amateur comedian and he appeared on stage at Post Office socials and local clubs. He had a fox called Jack which he reared from a cub. He also had three terrier dogs. Jack (the fox) was hired by a film company to appear in the film the "The Escape" with Sir Gerald Dumaurier, and when Jack died, Ernest was never was able to rear any more cubs. Ernest was a great walker and often took part in the London to Brighton walks; the family would drive him down to Brighton and he would then walk back as training. He was one of the first people to ride a penny-farthing bicycle and was an ice skating champion.

When he retired, he and his wife Clara returned to Crowland. He still had his bicycle from the Post Office which had a carrier on the front and he used to put a cushion in it so a small child could sit in it.

I remember feeding my grandparents' chickens. One was a Rhode Island Red called Mary-Anne Elizabeth and another a White Leghorn called Maria Jane Julia. Come Christmas dinner, I heard my Grandfather telling my mother that they were about to have Mary-Anne Elizabeth for dinner. Needless to say, I would not have any chicken on my plate.

Ernest Middleton died, aged 86 years old, in 1953.

Reminiscences.

My Maternal Grandfather
by
Irene Challenger. (HIS GRAND DAUGHTER)

ERNEST MIDDLETON
1867 - 1953

When I was quite small, my Grandfather used to joke with me, saying, 'If you have a headache, put your head through the window and the 'pane' will be gone'. One reads often these days, that old-age bring an inability to remember what was said only a moment ago, but ease in recalling & recounting, with great clarity, something that happened 50, 60 or even 70 uears ago. And isn't that the truth ? Now being seventy years 'plus', I get such detailed 'pictures'of childhood happenings, of things I was told, which happened years before that, with a clarity which truly amazes me . And Yes, , in the middle of a sentence , the word, I was about to say, has completely gone from my mind!

There's no doubt that my Mother's Father was a most personable character, humorist, athlete, sportsman, country-type, solid citizen and a very contented human-being. Born in CROWLAND Lincolnshire , the eldest son of a family of nine, his Father drove the Mail cart to and from the City of Peterborough, nine miles away, until one day, the horses slipped on an icy road, and he was thrown head-first off the cart and killed, at only forty two years of age. However, his Mother was allowed to keep the postal contract, so she hired a Driver ,but cared for the horses and the rest of the business herself and worked very hard to maintain her family. So, Grandfather when not yet fourteen, left home to live in the City, to join the Postal Service, as a telgram delivery 'boy', later becoming a Postman(Mailman) , then a Sprter of the Mail, until he retired at the age of sixty. I can 'see' him now, when I was just a toddler, both hands 'curling' each end of his 'handlebar' moustache, saying ,"your Grandad's name is Ernest Hardy Middleton, Born in the year of Our Lord, one thousand, eight hundred and sixty seven!" A very happy person, he had lots of hobbies. He was an amateur comedian appearing onstage at Post Office socials & other local Clubs, his favorite 'act' was to be dressed in Parson's hat & collar,and standing with head on one side,'pince nez' on his nose and clasped hands in front, he would recite monologues. Grandfather's fellow worker, Watson, took up professional entertainment, he became known as 'NOSMO KING', and was heard often on British Radio between the Wars. Grandfather told me, rightly or wrongly, that his friend got the idea of that name one day, when he was walking beside a passenger train on the station platform, and reading the 'No Smoking' signs on the train windows ! His son, Jack Watson, later had along career on British stage and radio, and lthen television, I believe.

Ernest Hardy, bred terriers, both the wire-haired and smooth coated types, He used to write his name down for me, with D.D., after it, laugh and say that means Dog Doctor. He had, also, a tame fox named 'Jack', and as a schoolgirl, I used to take Jack on a lead with several of the terriers too, for a walk into the local recreation ground, (Park). I'm sure 'Jack' didnt know he wasn't a dog, well he was a 'dog-fox ' anyway! In his later years, 'Jack' became famous as a film-star! A Film Conpany making the movie, 'The Escape' with Sir Gerald du Maurier, hired 'Jack' as the fox in a hunting scene, running infront of the hounds and Huntsmen. Grandfather explained to me later, that 'Jack' was not in any danger, as he ran on an extension wire, along another long wire and was out of reach of the 'Pack'. Grandfather used to run, on foot, behind the Fitzwilliam hounds at local 'Cub hunts', so that is how he obtained fox-cubs, but strangely enough, after 'Jack' died, he was never able to rear another.

He loved walking races, 'heel and toeing' and entered races until quite a good age. I remember him competing in local sports meetings when I was at school, he must have been in his early sixties and was still 'heel and toeing' it ! He kept a labge 'scrapbook' of press clippings of his 'walking' experiences. This included the story, of him competing in the fifty mile 'London to Brighton' walk just before World War I, when he was nearer fifty than forty, and he finished too. My Mother used to say, that for training before that race, he would go down to London on a train and walk the 78 miles home again! One day when competing in a local walking race and was way ahead of the other 'heel and toe' competitors, a woman spectator cried out "What a remarkable man' so his sister Emily Jane and her daughters (my Mother's cousins) who were watching at the time, hearing this, have since then, always talked of him as 'Our Remarkable'.

72

3.

GRANDFATHER WAS ONE OF FIRST TO OWN & RIDE A 'PENNY-FARTHING BICYCLE'. ALSO, HE loved to race, and was East Midlands Ice-skating Champion for many years, when there were 'icy winters ' in the fens, to allow for those competitions. On one such occasion, he fell on the ice and my Grandma, who had lent him her watch, knowing he had it in his top pocket, cried out, as he fell- "Oh my watch". This was a favorite family story between my Grandfather and my Mother for many years! Once, whilst competing in an ice-skating race on the fens, he fell on some 'Cat-ice' (I'm told), cutting his face very badly and he had many, many stitches, in his chin, lips, nose and upper cheeks, but his flesh healed so well, one could hardly see the scars, and he never lost one tooth ! He still had, all but one, very worn down to half the original height in front, from cracking nuts, and chewing on bones! He passed-on at the age of 86, although for years, as he sprinkled salt from a spoon, all over his dinner , he would say 'I'm going to live to be one hundred' y'know ! The brightness and good humor never left him, he was always full of cheer, would raise his hat to the ladies, though, understandably, a bit slow in the legs, he still walked the fifteen minutes each way to Church on a Sunday evening.

We all of us can sympathise with the feeling which comes, when getting older & not being able to compete , so too with Grandfather, he just couldnt bear the thought of not taking part in 'the action' but he got there anyway in mid field! Donning the white coat of the 'Starter', he volunteered to start the races at many local sports meetings. So, still in the public eye, his ego was fed, his name and photo appearing quite often in the local newspapers, and not only on the sports page, as local sports meetings often took position on the front page, when being one of the main items of public interest. Being to him the son and Grandson, he never had, I was brought up amongst all kinds of sports including soccer matches, not only with my Father but Grandfather too. Right up to the time of his death in 1953, when amongst local sports-minded people, I only had to mention "My Grandfather, Ernie Middleton" to suddenly trigger a contest of who could remember him in the most interesting story of/him, whether walking, ice-skating, following the hounds, or rabbiting or badger hunting with his dogs in the country etc etc.

After he retired and they had returned to live at Crowland, where he was born, he still had a very heavy bicycle like the letter carriers use, with a heavy, large, square-shaped carrier on the front. So as a small child, with an added cushion and support straps, I would ride on this, whilst he rode the bicycle, with shot-gun strapped under the cross-bar, and with the back carriers carrying boxes of ferrets, then the dogs would be running alongside and off we went, rabbiting or badgering, or sometimes wood-pigeon shooting. He would sell enough to pay for his cartridges. But both of my Grandparents loved pigeon pie, but they never persuaded me to eat any! I would feed Grandma's chickens sometimes, and I knew that she had names for the two large ones, one was a Rhode Island Red called, Mary-Anne Elizabeth, the other a White Leghorn, called Maria Jane Julia. Come one Christmas dinner, I heard Grandfather telling my Mother that We were about to have Mary-Anne Elizabeth for Xmas dinner ----- needless to say I wouldnt have not one piece of chicken, even, put on my plate!

Crowland was a very history-packed, small town, called a town because it had a market place. Crowland Abbey, St Guthlacs, (famous in a story about Hereward the Wake crossing the marshes and hiding in the Abbey) had only one remaining nave, the other two of the original three, were destroyed by the Cannon-balls fired by troops of Oliver Cromwell's soldiers, or so I was always told. I loved my school holidays there and played bowls with Grandfather and his friends. The bowling green was just the other side of the stone wall of the graveyard in front of the Abbey. A wonderfully restful scene; I can still 'see' it now, in 'my mind's eye'. --- I remember also, that every few years or so, Crowland would put on a Pageant, it was held in the field behind the Abbey, and Grandfather was always one of the marauding Danes (complete in horned helmets and furs) who would come swooping down, after jumping the stone wall! One of the most important jobs, preparing for the Pageant, was to clean up that field beforehand, where the cows had been grazing! I would walk there with Grandfather, pushing his wheelbarrow. One year, someone took a snap of us, complete with wheelbarrown and whenever I look at this, I just cant help laughing. The load of 'cow-slips' as Grandfather called it, believe me, smelt nothing like the flower of that same name!

When I was old enough to ride my own bicycle over to Crowland, Grandfather used to allow me to take over 'his job'. The PostOffice there, had no telegram delivery boy, so Grandfather had offered to do it. He would be told when there was a delivery and would ride out with it, to any nearby farm or wherever. for which he was paid fourpence per mile. So I just loved this, for just two miles each way, on my bike, I would receive the grand sum of one shilling and fourpence. A lot of pocket-money for me in those days, the early thirties !. Naturally his Grand-daughter took every opportunity to 'pull' Grandfather's leg about this, that he started out as a youth over fifty years ago, delivering telegrams, and was still doing it, no progress whatsoever ! Ha ha.

Crowland's other tourist attraction is its triangular (triangular) bridge. Sitting at the edge of the market place, it is the 'meeting' place of the four main streets of the town when one walks under it - No river, although there might have been, by some ancient drawings of it. The streets joining there, are North, South, East and West streets. We used to say, coming from the city, that Crowland was one of those places, which 'the Lord started' and had never finished! However, in later years as almost everywhere, increased population forced the building of new housing estates, and by-pass roads around the town. But in my school-days, the Ice-cream lady walked, pushing her barrow along the streets, stopping for any young customers running up to buy a 1d wafer, or a ½d cornet ! The Dairy lady lived only about three doors from my Grandma, who would say "It must be near 4 o'clock, look up the street and see if the cows are coming home." No-one had to fetch them in, after grazing, free all day on the open 'wash (or common), they would make their way home alone, knowing that it was milking time. Also, when I heard the first ring of the Town Crier's bell, I would go outside to listen. He would call out with each ring of the bell, "Oh Yea, Oh Yea, Oh Yea", the message being something, like - "Mr Green needs Peapickers for tomorrow, his lorry will be at the Town bridge at 5 a.m in the morning." etc etc.

6.

In later life, my Grandparents came back to live in the City, nearer to us. Then finally after my Grandma had passed on, Grandfather came to live with us. He would ride his bicycle out to the country, and I remember one night, that my Mother was so annoyed with him. He was late returning, and she was waiting with great impatience, to get dinner over and go to the local Theatre Royal, and she wanted him to go with her. So giving him no time to change, he was still in his 'hunting' clothes, when they arrived at the Theatre, only to find there were no Circle seats left as such, but they were seated in a Box, what could be called the Royal Box -- my Mother was so embarrassed, she never let her Father forget this occasion, and what's more the real point in this story, is that the title of the play they went to see performed, was "One damn thing after another ". Ha ha. Speaking of Mother, she was Ernest Hardy's only child and was christened Laurel, and would tell you, her favorite color was green. We would as a family, all enjoy going to the 'pictures' (the movies) and the Laurel and Hardy comedies were very popular and very often shown as the support movie. Well, one evening, Mother had gone to see her Doctor, he always made some comment about her 'evergreen' name. So this particular evening, he said " Laurel eh? Well then, where is Hardy?" So she answered immediately, smiling back at him, saying "Hardy ? Oh I left him at home !"

What personalities !

What happy childhood memories !

What wonderful times!

Charles Middleton in Stamford, Lincs

CENSUS OF ENGLAND AND WALES, 1911.

	NAME AND SURNAME	RELATIONSHIP to Head of Family	AGE last Birthday	PARTICULARS as to MARRIAGE				PROFESSION or OCCUPATION			BIRTHPLACE	NATIONALITY	INFIRMITY
			Males / Females	State Married, Widower, Widow, or Single	Completed years present Marriage	Children born alive	Children still living	Children died	Personal Occupation	Industry or Service	Employer, Worker, or Own Account			
1	Charles Middleton	Head	44	Married					Foundry Labourer	Engineering Works	Worker	Stamford Lincs	British	
2	Ellen Horence Middleton	Wife	43	Married	14	5	5	0				Stamford Lincs	British	sick by hæmorrhage
3	Louisa Ellen Middleton	Daughter	13						School			Stamford Lincs	do	
4	Constance Hermia Middleton	Daughter	10						School			Stamford Lincs	do	
5	Winifred Elizabeth Middleton	Daughter	5									Stamford Lincs	do	
6	Donald John Hedley Middleton	Son	2									Stamford Lincs	do	
7	Charles Raymond Middleton	Son	8 months									Stamford Lincs	do	

Signature: Charles Middleton
Postal Address: 31 Wharf Rd, Stamford, Lincs

Edward Thomas Middleton in Stamford, Lincs

CENSUS OF ENGLAND AND WALES, 1911.

Name and Surname	Relationship to Head of Family	Age (Males/Females)		Particulars as to Marriage					Profession or Occupation			Birthplace	Nationality	Infirmity
		Age Males	Age Females	Condition	Years Married	Children Born Alive	Children Still Living	Children Who Have Died	Personal Occupation	Industry or Service	Employer/Worker/Own Account			
1. Edward Thomas Middleton	Head	26		Married	3	3	3	0	Moulder Agricultural (Iron)			Stamford Lincs		
2. Gertrude Middleton	Wife		25	Married	3							Kate Northampton		
3. Francis Absolom Middleton	Son	3										Stamford		
4. Jane Elizabeth Middleton	Daughter		2									Stamford		
5. Gertrude Ellen Middleton	Daughter		2 mth									Stamford		

Totals: Males 3, Females 3, Persons 5

2 Bedrooms, 1 Living Room

Signature: Edward Thomas Middleton
Postal address: 2 Layton Brook Water Street Stamford

George Middleton in Stamford, Lincs

CENSUS OF ENGLAND AND WALES, 1911.

Name and Surname	Relationship to Head of Family	Age (Males)	Age (Females)	Particulars as to Marriage	Children Born Alive	Children Still Living	Children who have Died	Profession or Occupation	Industry or Service	Employer, Worker, or Own Account	Working at Home	Birthplace	Nationality	Infirmity
1 George Middleton	Head	57		Married				Brewers Labourer				Easton Northampton		
2 Sarah Jane Middleton	Wife		57	Married 22	2	2	No Children			at Home		Duffield Lincolnshire		
3 Cornelia Russell	Lodger		58	Single				Charwoman Rough & Ready	Private	At Home	0	Gt Paxton Lincolnshire		
4 Richard Middleton	Brother	49		Single				Farm Labourer		Worker C.C.		Tinwell Rutland		

4 Rooms House

Signature: George Middleton
Postal Address: Tinwell, Rutland

George Middleton in Stamford, Lincs

CENSUS OF ENGLAND AND WALES, 1911.

NAME AND SURNAME	RELATIONSHIP to Head of Family	AGE and SEX		PARTICULARS as to MARRIAGE				PROFESSION or OCCUPATION				BIRTHPLACE	NATIONALITY	INFIRMITY
		Males	Females	State	Years Married	Children Born Alive	Children Living	Children Died	Personal Occupation	Industry or Service	Employer/Worker	Working at Home			
1 George Middleton	Head	31		Married	8	1	1		Brewers Draymen	958			Stamford		
2 Jane Middleton	Wife		30		8	1	1						Uffington		
3 George Robert	Son	5											Stamford		

Total: Males 2, Females 1, Persons 3

4 rooms

Signature: Jane Middleton
Postal Address: 24 Emlyns Terrace
Water Street Stamford

Herbert James Middleton in Stamford, Lincs

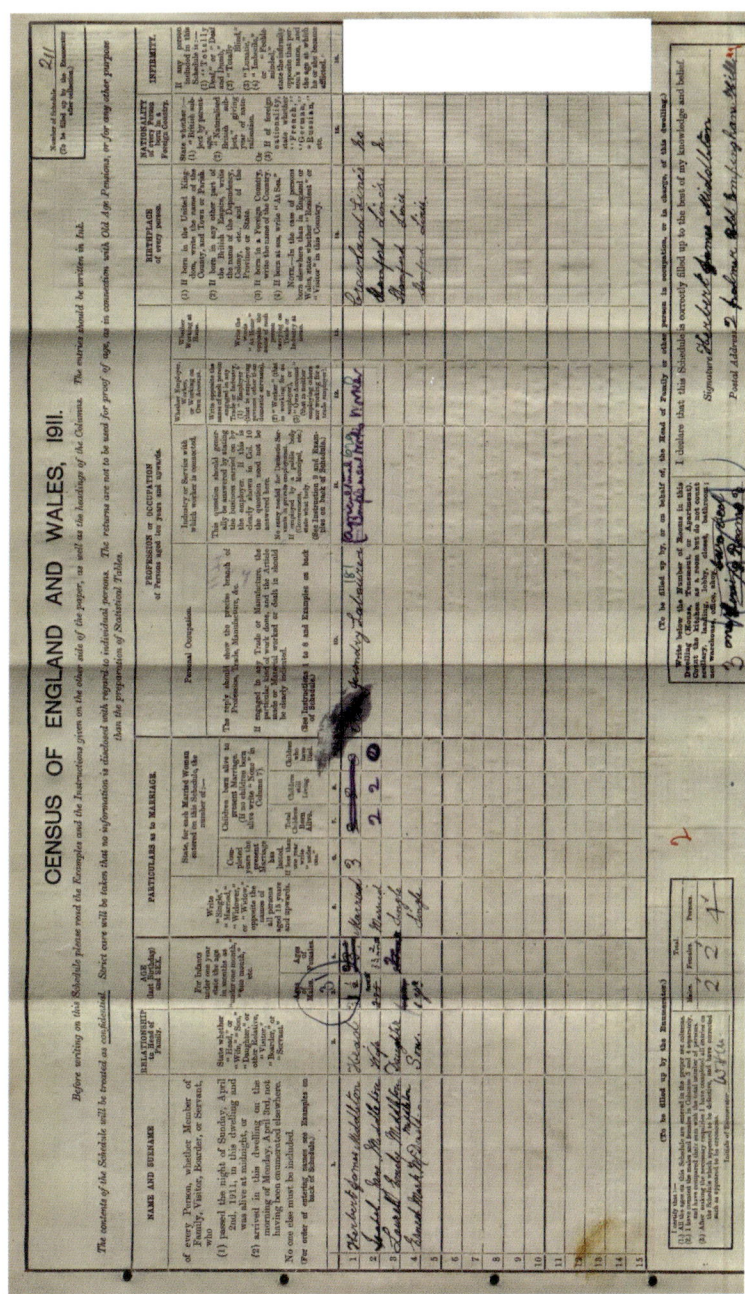

Edward Middleton in Stamford, Lincs

CENSUS OF ENGLAND AND WALES, 1911.

Name and Surname	Relationship to Head of Family	Age (Male)	Age (Female)	Particulars as to Marriage				Profession or Occupation	Industry	Employer/Worker	At Home	Birthplace	Nationality	Infirmity
				Condition	Years Married	Children Born	Children Living							
1 Edward Middleton	Head	38		Married	14	5	5	Iron Foundry Labourer		Worker		Lincolnshire Stamford		
2 Frances Emma Middleton	Wife		34	Married	14							Rutland North Luffenham		
3 Elizabeth Emma Middleton	Daughter		13	Single				General Servant				Leicestershire Uppingham		
4 Robert Edward Middleton	Son	11						Marine Store Assistant		Worker		Leicestershire Uppingham		
5 George Ernest Middleton	Son	9						School				Lincolnshire Stamford		
6 Nellie Middleton	Daughter		7					School				Lincolnshire Stamford		
7 Winifred Ellen Middleton	Daughter		10									Lincolnshire Stamford		
8 Gwendoline Ivy Middleton	Daughter		3									Lincolnshire Stamford		
9 John Arthur Leslie Middleton	Son	1										Lincolnshire Stamford		

Signature: Edward Middleton
Postal Address: 1 Elm St, Stamford, Lincolnshire

John William Middleton in Stamford, Lincs

CENSUS OF ENGLAND AND WALES, 1911.

Name and Surname	Relationship to Head of Family	Age (Last Birthday) and Sex		Particulars as to Marriage					Profession or Occupation			Birthplace	Nationality
		Males	Females	Condition as to Marriage	Years Married	Children Born Alive	Children Living	Children Died	Personal Occupation	Industry	Employer/Worker/Own Account		
1 John William Middleton	Head	50		Married	26	6	6	3	Moulder (Iron)	at Engineering	Worker	Stamford	British
2 Hannah Middleton	Wife		50	Married	26	6	6	3				Stamford	
3 Frank Middleton	Son	21		Single					Fitter		Worker	Stamford	
4 Amy Middleton	Daughter		24	Single					Servant (Domestic)		Worker	Stamford	
5 Edward Middleton	Son	23		Single					Labourer		Worker	Stamford	
6 Charles Middleton	Son	19		Single					Labourer		Worker	Stamford	
7 Fredrick Middleton	Son	17		Single					Errand Boy	Shop	Worker	Stamford	
8 John Thomas Middleton	Son	15		Single					Errand Boy		Worker	Stamford	

Signature: John William Middleton
Postal Address: 15 N Leonards St Stamford Lincs

5 rooms

Thomas Middleton in Stamford, Lincs

Name and Surname	Relationship to Head of Family	Age (last birthday) and Sex		Particulars as to Marriage					Profession or Occupation				Birthplace	Nationality	Infirmity
		Males	Females	Condition	Years Married	Children Born Alive	Children Living	Children Died	Personal Occupation	Industry or Service	Employer, Worker, or Own Account	At Home			
1 Thomas Middleton	Head	51		Married	26	4	4	none	Tailor & Draper (Shop Keeper)		Employer at home		Stamford Lincs		
2 Sarah Jane Middleton	Wife		51	Married	26	4	4	none					Netton Rutland		
3 Minnie Elizabeth Middleton	Daughter		24	Single					Assisting in the business	Tailor & Draper Worker	at Home		Stamford Lincs		
4 Thomas William Middleton	Son	22		Single					do	do	do		do		
5 Charles Frederick Middleton	Son	14		Single									do		

Signature Thomas Middleton
Postal Address 1 St Paul's St Stamford

Joseph Middleton in Stamford, Lincs

CENSUS OF ENGLAND AND WALES, 1911.

NAME AND SURNAME	RELATIONSHIP to Head of Family	AGE (last Birthday) and SEX	PARTICULARS as to MARRIAGE					PROFESSION OR OCCUPATION of Persons aged ten years and upwards			BIRTHPLACE of every Person.	NATIONALITY of every Person born in a Foreign Country.	INFIRMITY
		Ages Males / Females	Condition as to Marriage	Completed years the present Marriage has lasted	Children born alive to present Marriage (Total / Living / Died)			Personal Occupation	Industry or Service with which worker is connected	Whether Employer, Worker, or Own Account			
1 Agnes John Stephens	Head	52	Married	32	1	1	-	Builders Mason	Building	Worker	Leicester, Applethorpe		
2 Agnes Stephens	Wife	44	Married	32	1	1	-	—	—	—	Leicester, Castleton		
3 Joseph Middleton	Brother-in-law	44	Single					Clerk	Wheelwright factor Worker	050	Leicester, Castleton		

Write below the Number of Rooms in this Dwelling (House, Tenement, or Apartment). Count the kitchen as a room but do not count scullery, landing, lobby, closet, bathroom; nor warehouse, office, shop.

10

I declare that this Schedule is correctly filled up to the best of my knowledge and belief.

Signature: *James John Stephens*

Postal Address: *9 Fernando Street Stamford*

Total — Males 2 / Females 1 / Persons 3

Francis Middleton in Stamford, Lincs

CENSUS OF ENGLAND AND WALES, 1911.

Name and Surname	Relationship to Head of Family	Age (Males)	Age (Females)	Particulars as to Marriage	Completed years married	Children Born Alive	Children Still Living	Children Died	Profession or Occupation	Industry or Service	Employer/Worker/Own account	Working at Home	Birthplace	Nationality	Infirmity
Francis Middleton	Head	52		Married					Agricultural Labourer		Worker		Stamford Lincolnshire		
Janet Middleton	Wife		51	Married	32	8	6	2					Stamford Lincolnshire		
Elizabeth Middleton	Daughter		24	Married					Housewife				Stamford Lincolnshire		
William Middleton	Son	22		Single					Moulder		Worker		Stamford Lincolnshire		
Frank Middleton	Son	20		Single					Labourer		Worker		Stamford Lincolnshire		
Martha Middleton	Daughter		18	Single					Laundress		Worker		Stamford Lincolnshire		
Ellen Middleton	Daughter		12						School				Stamford Lincolnshire		
Dorothy Middleton	Daughter		9						School				Stamford Lincolnshire		
Francis Middleton	Son	6											Stamford Lincolnshire		

Signature: Francis Middleton
Postal Address: No 1 Rocksworth Buildings, St Leonards Street, Stamford

Chapter 4
Royal Mail in the 1800s

DRAWING OF A ROYAL MAIL CART

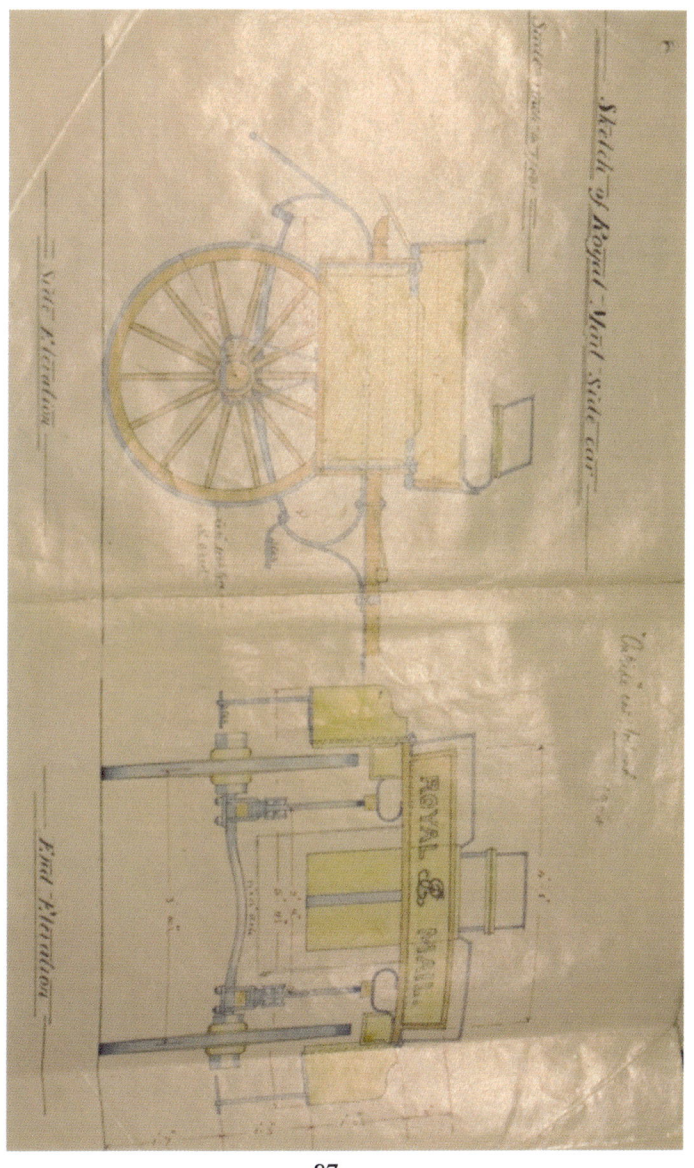

ROYAL MAIL CART DRIVER HAND BOOK
POST OFFICE REGULATIONS

POST OFFICE REGULATIONS.

ON AND AFTER THE 10th JANUARY, a Letter not exceeding HALF AN OUNCE IN WEIGHT, may be sent from any part of the United Kingdom, to any other part, for ONE PENNY, if paid when posted, or for TWO PENCE if paid when delivered.

THE SCALE OF RATES,

If paid when posted, is as follows, for all Letters, whether sent by the General or by any Local Post,

Not exceeding ½ Ounce	One Penny.
Exceeding ½ Ounce, but not exceeding 1 Ounce	Twopence.
Ditto 1 Ounce .... 2 Ounces	Fourpence.
Ditto 2 Ounces .... 3 Ounces	Sixpence.

and so on; an additional Two-pence for every additional Ounce. With but few exceptions, the WEIGHT is limited to Sixteen Ounces.

If not paid when posted, double the above Rates are charged on Inland Letters.

COLONIAL LETTERS.

If sent by Packet Twelve Times, if by Private Ship Eight Times, the above Rates.

FOREIGN LETTERS.

The Packet Rates which vary, will be seen at the Post Office. The Ship Rates are the same as the Ship Rates for Colonial Letters.

As regards Foreign and Colonial Letters, there is no limitation as to weight. All sent outwards, with a few exceptions, which may be learnt at the Post Office, must be paid when posted as heretofore.

Letters intended to go by Private Ship must be marked "*Ship Letter.*"

Some arrangements of minor importance, which are omitted in this Notice, may be seen in that placarded at the Post Office.

No Articles should be transmitted by Post which are liable to *injury* by being stamped, or by being crushed in the Bags.

It is particularly requested that all Letters may be *fully* and *legibly* addressed, and posted *as early* as convenient.

January 7th, 1840.

By Authority :—J. Hartnell, London.

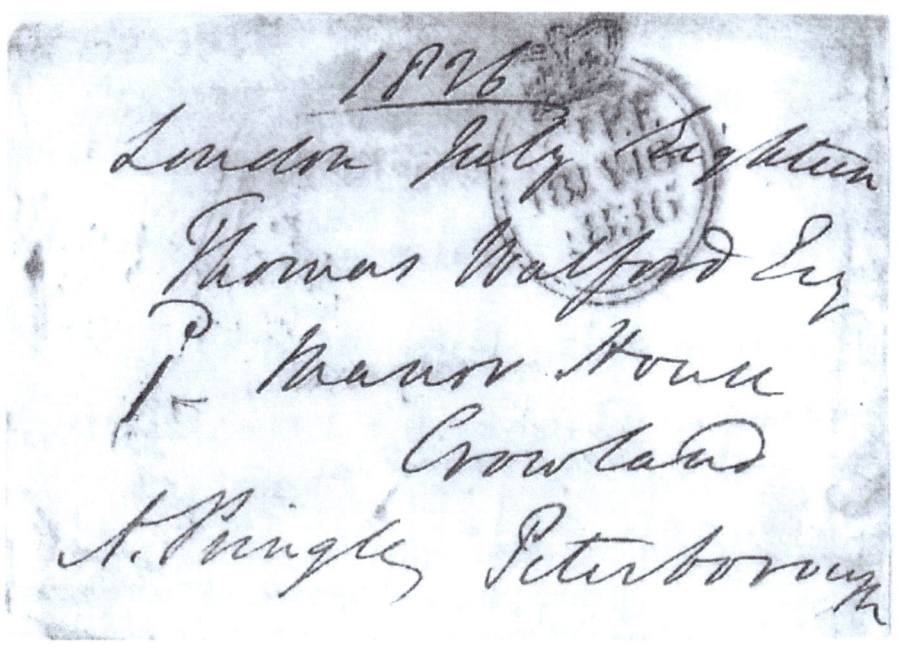

This letter is from London in 1836 sent by M.P. Pringle, name bottom left. The large printed circle with a crown on top, is the free mark (post free) put on in London, a privilege given to Members of Parliament, high-ranking army and naval officers, bishops and priests in high authority. The '1d' mark on the left, in ink, was a penny to take the letter from Peterborough to Crowland. We even know this was posted in the evening, by the double circle around the free mark.

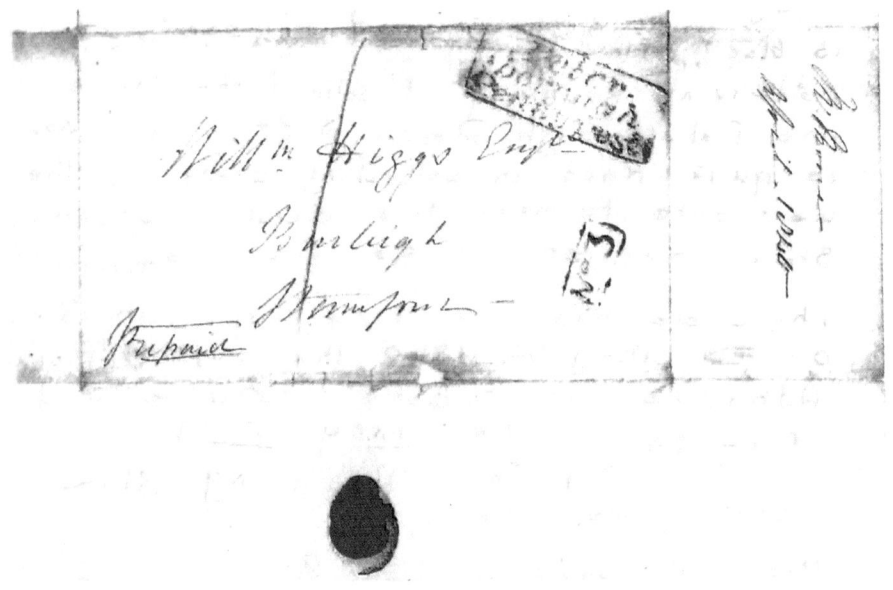

This letter has a number 3 in the square small box, which was the receiving house number from Crowland. The line straight through the centre - originally red - is denoting a 1d charge which was paid at this receiving house (bottom left). The stamp reading 'Peterborough Penny Post' in the big box (top right) is quite rare in collecting circles. It then went on to have the circular Peterborough stamp put on to go onto Stamford. The circle has the date 10th April, 1840.

On 6th May, 1840 the first official adhesive stamps came into use and on 8th May, the two-penny blue came into use. This letter would have been folded and sealed with red wax for security.

Some of the letters posted in the 1800s

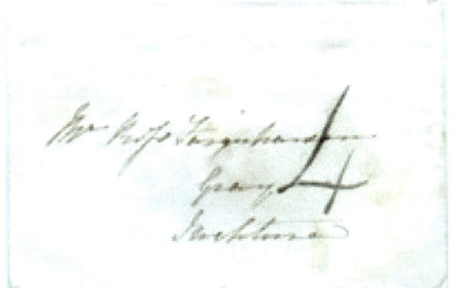

Chapter 5
Pictures of Mark Middleton and Family

Mark Middleton. Born 1842. Died 1883.

Freda Jennings (cousin) outside my grandma's house
(West Street, Crowland)
(Mark Middleton House)

George Taylor relief driver

The lower picture shows Crowland Post Office where Emma Middleton worked and above it, Mark Middleton, Emma's husband on his Royal Mail cart delivering mail. He was a mail contractor.

Mark Middleton   Robert Mark Middleton

Mark Middleton, born 1842, died 1883 with son Robert

Robert Mark Middleton (1875-1957). He was a bookmaker in Lincoln.

Emily Jane Butler (née Middleton)

Emily (née Middleton) & Ernest Butler

Great-grandmother Sharpe in the middle with grandfather Mark Middleton and grandmother Emma Middleton.
My mother Emily is between Mark Middleton's knees

Grandfather Sharpe

Grandmother Sharpe
(1802-1882)

My mam's mother (Emma) with second husband, John Hall
The first husband had been Mark Middleton

From right to left, front row:
Madeleine, Margaret, May and Percy Hall.

From left to right
Ernest Middleton, Emily Butler, Robert Middleton,
Ada (grandmother to Margaret Cary,) Gertrude Middleton,
Herbert Middleton, Sidney Hall.

Four Generations
Emma Hall (Middleton) maiden name Sharpe (died 1922), Ernest Hardy Middleton (son), Laurel Bend (née Middleton), Murial Bend

Sydney George Hall married Annie Ounsworth
in Lambeth, September 1907
Sydney b. Fylde, Dec 1908
Ethel A. Hall, b. Prestwick Mar 1913
Sylvia E, b. Bucklow 1915

Robert Middleton, son of Mark and Emma

E. H. Middleton restoring the Henry Girdleston Post, Postland Road, Crowland, about 1923

G. P. Strickland and E.H. Middleton
with his fox and the cup he gave for a football competition in 1923.
The fox went round on his shoulders, collecting for the medal fund.

Ernest Middleton with his
pet fox and dogs.

Ernest Middleton and relief
driver George Taylor.

Ernest Middleton 1867-1953
"The Remarkable" London to Brighton walker

Clara Middleton née Richards (Uncle Ernest's wife)

Gertrude Daffarn
Middleton

Laurel Emily Browning
née Middleton

Ernest Maiz McDonald Middleton, aged 77
Born 1910 Died 1992

30, Fulbridge Road
Peterborough,
PE1 3LA
18/2/2010

Dear Mr. John Kemmery,

I give my permission for the picture in the E.T. written by Mr. Percy Stanley Hall to be included in the book.

Mrs. M. A. Bros—

I hereby authorise that any Printed matter or Photographs of Historical Interest belonging to me, may be used by MR. J. KEMMERY.

Margaret Cary (Mrs)

1 St Mary Close
Crowland
PETERBOROUGH
PE6 0NR

01733 210435